SHAWANA, A MEMOIR

Shawana, A Memoir

BY SHAWANA THOMAS

Thomas Integrity, LLC

CONTENTS

DEDICATION

The first part of this book is dedicated to the people who taught me the importance of self-respect, integrity, spirituality, strength, peace, and love. To the strongest people I know, who did the best they could, when they could.

-My wonderful parents: Thank you both so much from the bottom of my heart for everything you've done to prepare me for life and for molding me into the woman I have become.

The second part of this book is dedicated to my two beautiful children:

- Terrell and Briana, you two have pushed me to always strive to be a better version of myself. You taught me patience, forgiveness, and true unconditional love. My love for you has helped me understand how much God must love us.

- I also want to thank my brothers for always being ready to listen to my poems and my husband for supporting me through this process.

I love and appreciate each and every one of you.

Introduction

I was born in October of 1983 and grew up on the south side of Chicago. If you're from Chicago and know anything about living on the south side in the 90s; you'd know about running when someone pointed and shouted "THERE GO HOMIE THE CLOWN!" You'd remember things like sliding down abandoned railroad tracks on garbage can tops, jumping double dutch with the other girls in the neighborhood, watching the boys do backflips on old thrown-out mattresses or play basketball - using crates they nailed to light poles for baskets, and waiting for someone to open the fire hydrants on those hot summer days. You may even remember your mom coming outside with a broomstick because you left the block or one of your neighbors tattled on you for doing something you had no business doing.

The south side is where I grew up and where I started writing. In the mid-90s, my parents were in their late twenties; my older brother was around thirteen, I was 11, my younger brother was 3, and my baby brother was a year old. I was always an analytical thinker; but sometimes, I would think myself into a place of low self-esteem and self-disappointment. My mom saw that I was struggling and purchased a diary for me - which I used often, to write my thoughts about the passing days.

When I was around the age of 13, my mom was cleaning out some storage and found an old poem she had written some time ago. *"Come here Shawana!"* she excitedly called me into her room,

"Listen to this poem I wrote a long time ago". I remember listening to her poem and thinking to myself, **wow, I wonder if I can do that?** Needless to say, my mom's poem was so beautiful, that it inspired me to also write poetry.

It wouldn't be until I was about 14 years old that I would write my first poem and sign it "Strawberry"; after that, I had a poem for almost every pivotal moment of my life - from the early age of 14, until I reached womanhood and had a family of my own. It only took me 24 years to finally put them all in one place; but, instead of just writing an ordinary book of poems, I wanted to do something a little different.

In this memoir, you will read the experiences from which the poems were derived. This includes experiences I had as a pre-teen, a teenager, a young woman, and an adult with a family of my own. My hope is that you receive the following message:

Please know that every decision you make will impact your life and it is up to you to make sure that every impact be a positive one. Trust in God to lead you in everything that you do and always operate out of love, integrity, and compassion for others. I hope you find my life experiences and their conjoined poems relatable, refreshing, and enjoyable to read.

~ I ~

THE BEGINNING

My parents' relationship was really strong. They were in their early thirties and you could see the friendship within their marriage very clearly. Although my parents didn't get married until my baby brother was in my mom's belly, they had been together since my mom was 16 and my dad was 19 years old. Growing up, I always noticed how they always had each other's backs, even against us kids, and we could forget about trying to put one parent against the other.

They were hustlers. My dad worked as a landscaper and had private clients. While my dad would be *outside* servicing the yard of a client; when she wasn't helping my dad, my mom would be *inside* caring for the elderly parent of the client. They called their company C&M Landscaping and were in business for quite some time. They were/are two of the strongest people with the biggest hearts you could ever meet. A pre-teen Shawana admired the love they had for one another, even in the times when my mom wouldn't be speaking to my dad and he would relay messages through me - although my mom would be in the next room and could clearly hear him. *(My mom's ignore game was strong)*.

3

My parents shared the same sentiments when it came to family; so, whenever a relative needed to stay with us for a while, my parents had no quarrels. There was nothing they wouldn't do for one another, and no one that could have broken them. They were truly a team in all aspects. 90s music like "All the Things" by Joe, and "Angel of Mine" by Monica; made me daydream about what someone loving *me* would be like, I was young, but I understood every lyric because of the love I saw and was inspired by every day with my parents.

The Perfect Fit (Written: 1998)

You stayed by each other's side no matter what,
through thick and through thin.
You two are lovers, sweethearts, valentines,
precious possessions to one another,
As well as very best friends.

God knew you two belonged together,
probably when your beds were just cribs,
And now there is joy in the both of you,
him knowing she shares his rib.

Together I watch you work with one another,
Both of you on one team.
and having a relationship like you two have,
Will always been my dream.

So stay together and continue to love one another,

Until death may do you part.
You are hers, and she is yours
Together, forever,
In soul, God's grace, and your hearts.

****

****

-A Dad Like You

In the Englewood neighborhood where I grew up, it was rare for a dad to be in the home. I can remember so many of my peers being shocked that my dad and mom were still together. At the time, I didn't understand what all the fuss was about, but it definitely made me appreciate my dad even more; because not only was my dad *in* the home, he was also very much a part of our lives. I can remember being around 10 years old or so, and listening to him get ready for work in the early morning hours. "My Mind Playing Tricks On Me" by the Geto Boys, would be blasting in the background and he would be rapping every word; eventually, I learned the entire song and would rap quietly along with him in my bed; until, I would hear the radio shut off, the front door open, then close.

When he would arrive home from work, my brothers and I would rush to the front door to greet him, and in a soft and tired voice he would say *"Yawl, give me a minute, let me get myself together."* That meant that he wanted to wash the day off and relax his mind after a long hard day of work. Once he did though, he and my brothers would be wrestling about the living room, while my mom finished cooking dinner. Whatever my dad could do to make us smile, he would do; from the trips to "Great America", to the "Chicago" "Down" coat he came home one day and surprised me with. On the mornings when he didn't have to work, he would wake us up to grits, eggs, bacon, and toast, and him shouting "ALL LITTLE RATS UP OUT THEY HOLES."

But, as soft and loving as my dad was with his kids, he was just as hard when it came to our education. As we got older, his phrase became "When you turn 18, that's your ass high-top!" this meant that we had better be doing something to ensure our futures because we couldn't just depend on him and my mom when we became adults. This taught us responsibility and independence, and while we knew we could always count on our parents; we were determined to not have to do so. My parents were very open with us, and my dad didn't sugarcoat anything. The most important lesson he taught us was to never let anyone knock us off of our square, *"Not even me or your mama,"* he would add.

A Dad Like You
(Written May 5, 1999)

Jesus blessed me with my Daddy,
and a wonderful man is he,
He's everything I pray and hope,
My husband will come to be.

He didn't run out on his family,
He was there before our lives began.
He is my wonderful, amazing daddy,
And also my best friend.

When I am down, he lifts me up,

And is always there to make me laugh
My dad gives his entire heart,
and never selfishly gives half.

Children with dads like mine vary,
There are barely just a few,
I just so happen to be one of them,
And I am very blessed to have you.

****
****

-A Letter to the Lord (Dedication to Mom)

While my dad was big on education, my mom was big on teaching us how important it was/is to have a relationship with GOD. I grew up listening to my mom blasting and singing gospel music on Sundays as she cooked dinner and cleaned the house. I remember a time when I was singing "As Long as I Got King Jesus" by Vicki Winans, and my older brother began laughing and teasing me. My mom yelled, *"Boy! Be quiet! She is shouting and praising the Lord!"* My mom always spoke about the goodness of the Lord and when the time came for us to get baptized; my mom, who had not learned to drive yet, had my dad take us to different churches every Sunday-trusting in the Lord to tell her which church was *the* one. We were baptized at New Friendship Baptist Church.

By the time I was 14, my older brother who was 16, had fallen in love with the streets. My younger brother was 8, and my baby brother was 6. My mom was spiritually growing and with every inch of her growth, she made sure she educated us as well. *"It's not about religion,"* She would say, *"It's about having a personal relationship with God."* We were no longer Baptist church members, we were Christians.

I watched my mom grow into a woman of God and I heaved every word that was given to her by HIM. I truly appreciate my mom and how she mothered, loved, and spiritually protected her children. I didn't realize it at the time, but I'm sure it was really hard and disappointing for her to see her firstborn and oldest son going in the direction he was going in. *"I just have to give him to the Lord,"* she would say. I didn't fully understand the magnitude of what that meant until I had children of my own. It meant that for every worry, heartache, and disappointment she had as a result of my brother's decisions, she was giving it all to the Lord; because it had become too much for her to bear on her own.

****

****

Dedication:
My mom set my spiritual foundation at such an early age, which is why this next poem is dedicated to her.

Thank you, mama, for planting the seeds for me to know, love, and trust in the Lord, even before I had my own personal experiences. Because of you, by the time I started going through the twists and turns of life, I already knew who to turn to.

Love Always,
-Shawana

A Letter to The Lord
(Written: 1998)

Dear God,
thank you for everything that you've done for me,
And everything that you'll do,
For I know,
my only reason for being on this bountiful earth
Is only to serve you.

You are my alarm clock, Lord,
you wake me each morning to your day,
It is you I love; you I serve,
Lord,
It is to you to whom I pray.

From a baby, to a toddler, to a teenager,
you have continued to be in my life,
And I know you will continue to guide me to be,
A virtuous woman, a loving mother, and wife.

I know that from you, My Father,
Is where I get the wisdom,
and strength to conquer life's maze,
Thank you Lord for being there for me,

Forever and Always.

~ II ~

THE MIDDLE (TEENAGE YEARS)

-Something Off Chest

By the year 2000, my parents had purchased their first home on the Southeast side of Chicago. I was in the middle/end of my freshman year of high school and was now living closer to my new friends. When I turned 15, my dad talked one of our neighbors into getting me an interview at Jewel Osco on 95th and Stony Island. I had been working there for about a year when I met "him".

I was 16 years old and had nothing going on in my life to write about, at least not until I had my first encounter with an older yet young man who made me feel something I had never felt before. One night, while at work, this man came in and had chosen to bag for me. I was a cashier, and every cashier would have someone to bag the groceries after they were rung up at the register. I remember thinking to myself **oh my goodness, who is that?** I could tell the girl at the cash register across from me shared my thoughts because she grinned at me as he made his way to my register.

"He" was about 5 feet 7 inches tall, muscular built with a brown sugar complexion, and had a low haircut with waves in his hair. He was super handsome and all the girls were digging him just as much as I was. Every time he would work while I was working, he would be my bagger and we would talk and get to know each other. About six months later, one Saturday, he and I had the same shift; so, once we were off of work he asked me to walk with him, instead of standing at my usual bus stop. I obliged, and we came across a church that had empty church buses parked in the parking lot. The doors to one of the buses were unlocked; so, he pried them open and guided me up the steps and onto the bus. (don't judge me.) Anyway, I was so nervous but so curious about what this man; who had already graduated high school, was about to introduce me to.

He held my hand as he guided me to the back of the bus then used his body to lie mine down on the seat. He took off my coat and lifted my blouse with one hand as he kissed my neck and touched my body in ways I had never felt before with the other, I liked it, and even though it was freezing cold I wanted more. He began kissing my stomach and had made it all the way down to the bottom of my belly button, when the fear and the fact that we were in a church bus, behind a church, made me feel something awful and uncomfortable.

I asked him to stop and shared with him that I was a virgin and didn't want my first time to be on the back of a church bus. *"Let me just kiss it"* he pleaded. *"No"*, I responded, *"Not here"*. He kissed my neck one more time before allowing me up. I wanted to run off the bus as fast as I could; but, not wanting to look immature, I kept my composure. My mind raced from the time I got off *that* bus until the time hopped on my regular bus and arrived home. *What was this feeling?*

Something Off My Chest (Written: 2000)

There is something very strange coming all over me,
Too hot to handle,
And too vague to see.

I have no idea in mind about what I should do,
One, continue my own way,
Or two, follow you.

I admit, you leave me curious, and I admit, it does feel good,
But taking it all the way with you,
I'm not really sure if I should.

And then, there's a little voice in the back of my head,
Telling me how far I came,
Reminding me of the consequences
That comes along with this game.

And so I think, what's going to happen?
if I tell you that I will.
The one true thing, that is kept for my God,
My body,
to you,
I cannot give.

-What I Want in a Man

-The Relationship Rose

I had just had a taste of what a sexual encounter with a man would feel like and definitely needed reinforcements. My mom didn't know about the encounter I had; but, she knew something was going on and purchased me a Trinity 5:7 CD - to listen to in my times of weakness. My favorite song was "My Body is the Lord's Temple". I listened to that song all the time and it truly gave me strength. Although I started to think about sex a lot, I also started to think about a relationship.

I began soaking up everything I saw in the relationships around me; this included the many relationships my older brother had, my parents' marriage, and my aunts' and uncles' relationships and marriages. I started to visualize what kind of man I wanted, and how I wanted to be treated. I was also the only girl in my nuclear family and had an over-protective dad and older brother; so, I knew what it felt like to be loved and protected, and I wanted those same characteristics in my romantic relationships as well.

What I Want in a Man (Written: 11/20/2001)

I want a man who is strong with his hands,
But always gentle is he.
Who is strong in the chest and does his best
in anything that pleases me.

Who says the right things to lift me up,
And is always by my side.
One that I run to -when I am distressed,
His arms are open wide.

I want a man, a man not a boy,
Who does not like to play games.
Together we'll grow, together as one,
Good- always our change.

One that I can tell my problems to
and things I may go through
One who I can feel safe,
to openly say
those special words....
I.. Love... you.

The Relationship Rose (Written: 2001)

From its underground, it is planted,
From one simple seed.
On its' pedals wishes granted.
Rain and sun its' need.

It starts from roots that spread
And underground they grow,
Poking out its beautiful head,
Then, from its home, it rose.

Blooming wings of color,

A bright and beautiful red
And not just for passion and endearment,
More love and hope instead.

A rose is like a relationship,
It starts from a simple seed.
Each other's wishes granted,
Except, love and trust its' need.

You start from roots that spread,
Together you change and grow,
You'll bloom as time is led,
Just like that beautiful rose.

So nurture your relationship,
In all that you may do,
And get yourselves a nice red rose,
So it can grow with you.

****

****

It was the beginning of my senior year of high school. My Trinity 5'7 CD had kept me away from "him", and got me closer to one of my high school classmates, who like me, was also a Christian. He was intelligent and had goals and aspirations of his own and I was feeling pretty good about the relationship. We had been good friends since our sophomore year and had even agreed to attend prom together. We started "talking" our Junior year but stopped shortly after; however, our feelings for one another were still very evident.

It was now our senior year and he asked me out on a date for that upcoming Saturday, I accepted with no hesitation. I was at the highlight of my high school career: My GPA was good, I was waiting on college acceptance letters, I had a decent group of friends, and my family was healthy and well. The only thing that was missing in my life at that time, was a boyfriend *(and I really didn't even care about that.)* Although it didn't work out in our junior year, "the classmate" and I were a bit older now and decided to give it another shot; either way, he was still going to be my prom date. My focus was on point and my life was heading in the direction I saw for myself.

Saturday morning came, and on that Saturday, September 22, 2001, my dad woke me up to the most devastating news of my life. My older brother was shot multiple times, and may not have survived. At that time, he was 20 years old, I was 17, my little brother had just turned 12, and my baby brother was about 10. I remember praying really hard for him not to die. I told the Lord that I would take care of him if he could no longer walk, and to just please don't take my brother. I didn't understand that I was praying for something that had already happened. My brother had already died around 5 am that morning. It was my senior year of high school, I was turning 18 in less than a month, and I lost my best friend in a horrific and unexpected way. Our family was devastated. My childhood and all the memories that came with it had become memories that I now had no one to share with.

That moment changed everything I thought about life. I stepped outside and cars and buses were still being driven, stop lights were still operating, and people were outside walking around like nothing ever happened. The world was still moving while my world had stopped. I couldn't believe the world was acting as though I didn't just lose a piece of my heart. I was so angry at God. Up until that moment I had two goals, serve God, and succeed; but, after that moment, I no longer cared about anything. I was living my life on auto-pilot, no longer caring if I lived or died. I tried my best to cope, but I had just spoken to my brother the night before and he was ripped out of my life so instantaneously and my brain was having a hard time processing it all.

My brother and I grew up together and were very close. When we were little, we would ride our bikes through the Holmes Elementary school parking lot to get to the arcade, where we would play street fighter. I would be Chun-li, and he would be either Ryu or Ken. Sometimes, we would even meet up with our friends, who were also brother and sister, and we would all sneak and ride our bikes on what we would call adventures.

Like most kids, we loved allowance Fridays. We couldn't wait for our dad to come home so we could walk to the candy store down the street and load up on sweets. We shared a room; so, once we had gotten our candy, chips, and juice, we would lie our blankets in front of our T.V. and watch the "Bullwinkle and Rocky" show. On school nights, we would be up all night talking about what happened in our classes. I lost my best friend in this entire world, how was I supposed to imagine life without him? I did the only thing I could think of, I wrote, and I wrote.

Marcus (Written:10/2001)

Every time I close my eyes,
This face appears to me.
This gentle stare without surprise,
And then, to me, he speaks.

He tells me not to be afraid,
Of what this world can do,
He says "your growing strong Shawana"
"I see the light in you"

He says "I'm fine, I'm in my place",
"exactly where I belong".
"No more hustling, no disgrace,
Here, I do no wrong."

This face so handsome, so dark and pure,
His eyes were so stern yet sweet,
This young man, whom I grew to know,
and means the world to me.

I'm listening to him as he speaks,
Me, taking everything in.
"This world", he says "was a hectic game,
A game I could not win"

Those words he spoke sunk into me,

And took over what was left of my mind.
I knew then, the strength in me,
Was now not hard to find.

"Cry for happiness," he said to me,
"weep for me no more,
And when our time comes to meet again,
I'll be waiting right by the door."

Life and Death

Life,
It comes and goes,
As quickly as a blink of an eye.
Some grow and age in wisdom,
But some,
prematurely die

Death,
It is a spirit,
not so sure if good or bad,
Being happy for a death so hard do,
so used to being so sad.

It can change your ways of thinking,
or make you wonder why you came,
It is the beginning of a whole new living,
And the ending to life's game.

-Uncelebrated Birthday

Four months had quickly gone by, and it was my brother's first posthumous birthday. Whenever January 8th would come around, my brother would call the house and say, *"Today's my birthday"*. I would always smile and say, *"Duh! Happy Birthday Pooh! What are you doing for your birthday?"*. "Pooh" was his childhood and family nick-name. He would answer, *"I don't know, probably kick it"*; we would roast each other, and laugh at our jokes, then, the phone would be passed to everyone who was in the house at the time of his call, and he would say the same thing, *"Today's my birthday."* My brother moved out of the house and began living the "street life" at the early age of 15, by the time he turned 16, he was already rooted in that life; so, he matured much faster than most kids.

This birthday was hard because, although I knew we wouldn't be getting that call, in some way, I still hoped that we would. I wasn't kidding when I said my brain couldn't process it. I literally was not excepting the fact that he was gone. I waited, hoping that it was all just a dream and the phone would soon ring with him on the other end saying, *"Today's my birthday!"* but of course, it never did.

Dedication:
Written: 1/8/2022

Uncelebrated birthday is dedicated to my big brother, Marcus Terrell Adams, born January 8, 1981, and died September 22, 2001. He would have been 21 years old today. I love you Marcus now and forever, until I see you again, you will always be in my heart. You are my heart and no one in this world can ever take your place as my big brother.

Love: Your Little Sister, Shawana

Uncelebrated Birthday (Written: 1/8/2002)

You lived your life unexpectedly,
Always full of surprises.
having many different personalities,
And many different disguises.

Trapped inside a wall,
and ready for it to break,
Not knowing what else to do,
Or how much more to take.

Putting on a front,
to those who knew you best,
Claiming you're having fun,
Saying "No time to rest".

Almost reached the golden age,
What people call "the life".
almost isn't good enough,
Almost isn't right.

I remember our conversations,
And all the things you kept inside,
And I remember your beautiful smile,
was behind doors were a help-filled cry.

I love you more than ever,
Even though you went astray.
I'm glad you have peace,

Now you have God

and that makes.... A happy Birthday..

****

****

-Words of Encouragement

It was now 2002, I was at the end of my senior year, and my GPA had dropped tremendously. I no longer cared about prom, or graduation because my brother was not there to share those moments with me. At that point, I had distanced myself from "the classmate" because I knew I was going in a totally different direction and I didn't want to drag him down the rabbit hole with me. You know how some people give themselves pep talks like *"You got this!" "You can do this"! "You are an amazing person and can accomplish anything you put your mind to."* I needed to regain my drive; so, instead of giving myself a pep talk, I wrote down words of encouragement to myself, speaking to the negativity in my brain. I knew that the enemy was using my sorrow and grief to keep me in a state of depression and anger, so I needed something to put me back in drive mode because I was definitely still on autopilot.

Words of Encouragement (Written 1/25/2002)

No matter how hard it may be,
for me to go from bad to best,
I'll do whatever I need to do,
to make sure I pass this test,
of strength, of endurance, of being me until I die.
Not letting the enemy get to me,
Not letting him make me cry.
Not letting him put me down or make me not care,
Not pounding me, not pressuring me, not hurting me,
Not knocking me off my square.
But keeping me, ME,
healthy, occupied, and strong,
Giving him no choice at all,
but to listen to my song,
Of love, of honesty, of joy, and glee,
Telling him that's why you're stuck with you
And I am blessed with me.
And while you're trying so hard to break me
I'm going to make sure I pass this test,
I'm going to make sure my bad gets better,
And I won't stop,
Until I reach my best.

~ III ~

A YOUNG WOMAN

I was an angry, unhinged 18-year-old whose mom had just bought a computer, and I found myself submerged in the internet *all* night. There was one social media platform in particular that I visited the most. It was kind of like the one that is popular today, except this one was geared more towards the black folks. One particular night I received a message from a guy who lived on the west side of Chicago. (Let's call him "West-side"). He and I exchanged phone numbers and began a so-called relationship. He was in college and spoke like a man who knew what he wanted, and I was impressed. He was about three or four years older than I was and seemed to be really mature.

We had been talking on the phone for about a month or two before I decided to meet him in person. I went to school on a Monday and told my friend I would be skipping school the next day to lose my virginity-*(yes, I had planned this, unbeknownst to "west-side")*. Tuesday came and I rode two trains all the way to his house. He met me at the second train station and neither of us was disappointed in the way the other one looked.

He was a lean guy, who stood at about 5'9, had a caramel complexion, and wore a do-rag that covered his low-cut hair. We walked to his apartment and went straight into his bedroom where he had pictures of me on a board attached to his wall, and saved as the background on his computer screen. He helped me take off my book bag and sat me down on his bed. *"Lie down,"* he said, as he lay beside me. *"Lay your head on my chest"*, he began combing his fingers through my hair. He spoke in a demanding tone that turned me on; so, in the middle of whatever it was he was saying, I began kissing his earlobe. He was trying to talk to me, but I was there on a mission, *"We have time for that,"* he said, but I wouldn't stop.

He eventually gave in and began kissing me back then stood up to remove his shirt. I asked him to get a condom, but he refused saying *"I don't use condoms."* If I were not doing this out of anger, I would have demanded he used one. My anger and rebellion against God clouded my judgment; nonetheless, this man took his time with me and made my first time something I would never forget.

My First Time *(Written: May 14, 2002, the day I lost my innocence)*

My first time was gentle,
Slow, romantic, and sweet.
His touch was soft, his kisses sensual,
Heated, from head to feet.

He rubbed my face, and kissed my lips,
Abyss, a bliss
My neck, my shoulders, my chest, my breasts,
Then softly, he kissed my wrist.

He looked into my eyes
while licking my body complete,
All around my belly button,
A feeling
I could not defeat.

Lying there so unafraid,
Though me being so pure,
I didn't think, that such little pain,
I'd only have to endure.

Afterward, we fell asleep,
Him holding me so tight,
If I could have, I promise I would have,
Stayed with him the rest of the night.

He made me feel so special,
With him, I felt so free.
Like we were alone on a deserted island,
And all he needed was me.

My first time was unforgettable,
definitely not just fling,
And if I can change it,
In any way at all,
I wouldn't change a thing.

****

****

-Only with You
-Double Dutch, Chocolate Fudge, Triple Scoops of Love

I fell in love with the art of sex after losing my virginity. Two bodies becoming one in a pool of intimacy, the satisfaction of pleasing one another, and the different angles and positions of pleasure. I loved every bit of it. The most insecure person could feel so sexy in the art of lovemaking. Just the thought of every touch and kiss turned me on.

I began craving the sexual gratification I was introduced to and would close my eyes and imagine my next encounter. What would it be like? whom would it be with and where? My imagination started to go places I knew nothing about. I was a fish fresh out of water with no experience whatsoever; so, I allowed my mind to take me anywhere it wanted while I just laid back and enjoyed the ride *(wink)*.

Only with You (Written:6/2002)

In the living room on the couch
Or upstairs in our bed,
candle wax, whip cream,
let strawberries be fed.

In the bathroom on the toilet seat,
Or in the shower dripping wet,
On the bathroom sink, dipped and spread,
Let both our needs be met.

In the kitchen on the table,
Or on the dining room floor
In the closet, peaches and cream
Let me keep yearning for more.

In the den against the television,
Or maybe on top of the stairs,
In the car, bananas and chocolate,
Let you be gasping for air.

In the bathtub full of bubbles
Or in the Jacuzzi swirl,
Lick my chin like cherries,
Let my toes be curled.

Wherever we decide to go
And whatever we decide to do,
Be sure to bring the fruit and more,

exotic, anywhere,
And let it only be with you.

Double Dutch, Chocolate Fudge, Triple Scoops of Love
(Written: 2002)

When I come home and see you there,
Waiting for me, your flesh is bare,
you remind me so much of double dutch.

You've got dinner placed for me, on a plate,
Yet, it is you I so desperately anticipate.
You're staring at me,
your eyes won't budge,
coloring my body with chocolate fudge.

Then to top it all off and put a cherry on top
You leading me towards the tub,
You ready for me?
I'm ready for your,
Triple scoops of love.

****

****

-*Reflection*

In June of 2022, after my high school graduation, I was in somewhat of a better place. I didn't go to prom; however, I didn't want my parents to miss out on the opportunity of watching their only daughter graduate from high school. I was able to look at myself and love myself again. I started to gain this confidence that I'd never had before.

There I was, 18 years old, and on my way to college, and not just any university, but *the* University. The only school I had ever wanted to attend. I felt like I was well on my way to achieving my dreams in spite of my pain, and although I was really mean to "the classmate," he and I were still really close friends. We still had an unspoken love for one another, but it was something I chose not to pursue. I was coming into my own; however, I was no longer the person I once was and I didn't want my choices to affect his life; not to mention, I was still in a "so-called relationship" with "west-side".

"West-side" and I had been "together" for a short while, and although I didn't see him or talk to him as much, this man had me wrapped around his finger. It was weird because he came to my graduation party and acted so uppity and entitled. He completely turned me off; but, I guess him being my "first" released some type of mild attachment hormones because whenever he would call, I would come. One day, when I was on my way to work in downtown Chicago, we ran into each other while getting off the L (train line). I said to myself, *"Don't you do anything, just act like you don't see him."* But, he spotted me amongst the crowd of people, and in his demanding tone he said, *"Come here"*, and I did, he said, *"Give me a kiss"*, and I did. URG! I had not heard from, or seen this man in weeks, and there I was, following his orders. He ended our transaction with a *"Call me when you get off of work tonight."*

I demanded myself not to call him, but deep inside I couldn't wait to get off work so I could, and when I finally did, he didn't even answer the phone. I never felt so stupid. I vowed to myself to break whatever hold it was he had on me and to never allow another man to have me like that again. I called him about a month after that encounter to give him a piece of my mind, and that's when he apologized for the things he had done in our so-called relationship and admitted that he never fell out of love with his ex and that they were expecting a baby.

It was closure, that I really didn't need seeing as how I had already moved on and was only still in Chicago until it was time for me to leave for college. If you can remember, a couple of pages back, I mentioned how success and my relationship with the Lord were my only goals. Well, I guess that part of me was still there somewhere because achieving graduation and being accepted to my dream University made me feel really good about myself. I was confident and ready to begin life as an adult, on my own.

Reflection (Written 7/10/2022)

Damn I love looking at this woman,
Her style as well as grace,
Her golden brown complexion,
And the angelicness of her face.

I love watching this woman walk,
The way she moves with pride,
She walk like she walking down a runway,
She has a sexy stride.

Her hair is so exotic,
Her eyes have this glow,
She keeps this look upon her face like,
You all just gots' to know.

Of her beauty, of her intelligence,
Of her strength and strong will to feel free,

But do you know, what I love most about this woman?
It's how she looks –
right back at me.

****
****

-Triangle

Let's go back a bit to the year 1998. I was 14 years old, a freshman in high school, and my mom had just told me that I can give one boy my phone number. Can you imagine what was going through my mind? a 14-year- old skinny girl, with no boobs, no body, and short hair? It felt good that I could finally give a boy my phone number. The feeling didn't last very long though, because I didn't have any boys interested in me enough to even *ask* me *for* my number.

One day, one of my best friends called me telling me about a boy she used to "go with" - when he called her on her other line. She clicked over and said, *"He wants your phone number girl, should I give it to him?"* We concocted a plan to make him fall for me, then

I break his heart as he did hers. The plan was going as expected, at least until he started calling me at 3:00 p.m. every day when he knew I would be out of school. I hadn't even seen him yet; but somehow, he drew me in with his personality, consistency, and sense of humor. One day, he called me and asked me if I wanted to see what he looked like; when I fearfully replied with a yes, he told me to turn my TV to channel 13, and there he was; this skinny light-skinned boy, with curly black hair. I was relieved at how cute he was. About a week later, I called my friend up and told her that I was falling for him, and after she gave her blessing, he and I were inseparable. We became so close, that my mom even allowed him to come over and hang out sometimes.

Fast forwarding to the year 2003, my 19-year-old self and "him" had become involved in our separate lives, but always remained best friends. He would pop in and out of my life from age 14 until we were about 20 years old, and I was there for every bit of it. This time though, he had popped in telling me about a girl he met and how he was falling in love with her. He wanted us to meet; so, he put her on the phone for us to introduce ourselves and she and I got along pretty well.

He was my first experience with loving someone in that way. *("Puppy love")* Regardless of what was going on in his life, he would always make sure to call me. Sometimes he would call - just to check on me, other times he would call - just to tell me he loved me, and most times he would call, and not say anything, but have "Sweet Lady" by Tyrese playing in the background. He and I had a mutual understanding, he was living his life, and I was not ready to give all of myself to him; so, we maintained our love and friendship and were there for one another when we needed to be. There was now nothing left for me to do but be happy for him, I was crushed because, at the time, I thought that meant the end of *our* relationship. I would later find out, I was wrong.

Triangle (Written: 2003)

I'm stuck inside of a triangle,
And I don't know what to do,
Because while you're falling in love with her,
I'm still in love with you.

You were my first love,
But yet, she is yours,
Mixed directions, we're together,
And a triangle is its course.

We were apart for one whole year,
And I didn't know what to do.
Every man that I befriended,
Were all compared to you.

And while you were busy finding out
That you were done with it all,
and wanted to make her your wife.
I was busy trying to contact you
Because I needed you in my life.

Then, when I thought I was over you,
You came back, saying you were home
Now, the feelings I thought I had dismissed,

I found were never really gone.

You don't seem to understand,
That you were my first love,
and it hurts that she is yours.
Mixed directions we're together again,
But a triangle is the course.

I'm the one stuck inside of this triangle,
And I don't know what to do,
Because while you're falling in love with her,
I'm still in love with you.

~ IV ~

ALL GROWN UP

In the next two years of my life, I started a new relationship that I'd been in for about a year at this point *(we'll get to this, just keep reading)*; three teenage cousins had moved in and joined our family, and I was attending school and had been on my job working for a messenger center for almost two years. I didn't get the chance to go to my dream University because my dad did not approve of its reputation, and since there was no plan B, I ended up just getting a job and attending a school in downtown Chicago. Life was too busy to write; until one night, my mom, aunts, cousin, and I decided to have a lady's night out. We ended up at a poetry gathering and I was introduced to a new form of poetry called- spoken word. I didn't know it at the time, but I had dibbled and dabbled in spoken word with my poem titled "Words of Encouragement" in chapter 1, but this was something different, this was spectacular.

All the poets were great, but there was one young lady who completely killed it! She is who inspired me to write my first "real" spoken-word piece. If you look back at my prior poems, they did not include any curse words or extremely provocative language. "Black Men" is a provocative piece that I did not hold back on. Although it was written in 2004, It made its' debut at a poetry event in Springfield, IL, in 2005 when a friend of mine had invited me out to an open mic event; and unbeknownst to me, had signed me up as a performer. I was super nervous when the DJ called me to the stage. *"Now coming to the stage, is a virgin on the mic."* I began looking around like "Uh oh, who's about to come up". *"Let's show her some love yawl!"* The crowd began to cheer *"Welcome to the stage..."* *Shawana!"* I thought I was going to pee my pants. I nervously looked at my friend who began approaching me. "It's okay," he said, *"you got this!"* I had recited the poem to him a week prior as he himself also wrote poetry, and with his encouragement, I got up on stage, took off my glasses to calm my nerves, and received an overwhelming response from the crowd.

Black Men (Written 2004)

I just love black men, love to touch black men,
love to rub, suck, and make love to black men-
My-
brown-skinned, light-skinned, and Hershey's chocolate
black men-they
make my body just oh.
I mean I love all shades of black men-
but my -
black-black men just do something to me, I don't know.
My strong and hard-working ass black man whose..
hands.... feel.... good... on me.
My-multi-talented black man- who can-
rub and touch, and suck and lick
every each and part of my body-
hardly breathing-
While my thick black man can manhandle my little ass-

and make me feel secure- his
mas-cu-linty got me- so....pleased.
Mentally, physically, and emotionally-
THAT MAN CAN -UCK THE SHIT OUT OF ME-
and make love to me at the same time
while my-
black women missing the feeling sitting,
complaining about good men being hard to find and
In my mind, I be thinking the same thing,
but that man got me thinking -
imma work with what I got because he – is - pleasing me,
on his knees slowly
eating me-
my ish from behind- kind of-
relaxing-
this attraction I have for my black men is so strong,
passionately long-lasting.
And I don't ask him no questions because he's got me so gone
he is-
forcing it off the tip of my tongue-
OH I-
LOVE MY
BLACK –MEN....and...
You ladies can look at me like girl please,
I disagree,
these men ain't really thinking about you-
and that - may be true-
but- it's okay- because I don't see them running away
so- I-
know I'm right when I say,
them -itches love black men too.

****
****

- *Can You See Me?*

Now, lets go back to the end of 2002, *before* my move to Spring-field in 2004. I had just turned 19 years old when I got into my first "real" relationship. He had been a friend of our family since I was about 14 years old; *(specifically, with my dad)*, and was older than me by about six or seven years. He was a hustler and had his hands in *many* different pots; *(in fact, let's call him, "The Hustler")*. He had a good job though and was very quiet about what he did in his past times. You had to have known him, and he had to have trusted you - for you to know him closely. I was young, and one of his past times consisted of business with other women; because of this, he suggested that we be in an open- relationship. *"You're young and I want you to still experience life,"* he said.

At first, I didn't like the idea, but after about a month or so, I started to entertain *and* enjoy it. I enjoyed telling him about the men that I would be "talking to", and I loved how he would tell women that he was with his girl (me)-when they called his phone. I experienced a totally different side of life with him and I liked every bit of it. He took care of me in all aspects; he kept me in the latest brands, and money in my pockets, and even bought me my first car. He was a master at his oral abilities. I was totally addicted to *that*, as well as the lifestyle of being with him. He was the first man I loved outside of "puppy love"; but, because our relationship was open, I didn't have room to actually fall *in love* with him.

Nonetheless, everything was going great, until after about 6 months into the relationship, when he tried to control whom I dated and what I did. The open relationship was fine; however, if I spoke about one guy for too long, "The hustler" would no longer be "okay" with me spending time with said guy. This didn't go well with me because I absolutely disliked being controlled. I promised myself that a man would never have me wrapped around his finger again, and I was not about to break that promise for anyone.

His control tactics were very manipulative and although I wouldn't show it, they would sometimes leave me confused and feeling helpless. He did things like, not talking to me for weeks; or, answering the phone then hanging it up again when I called; one time, he called me to come over to his house, just so he could not be there when I got there. I was so discombobulated, that I accidentally drifted my car into a light pole on my way back home. *(Thankfully, I didn't hit it very hard).* He did all those things just because I did something he didn't want me to do, or saw someone he no longer wanted me to see. At that time, I didn't realize the mental abuse I was enduring because I felt somewhat vindicated in the ways that I would lash out at him. Whatever he didn't approve of, I did even more and made sure he knew about it.

A year and a half into the relationship, I found out I was pregnant. I was so scared and didn't know how I would tell my parents. My mom seemed to have known as soon as I walked through the door, she was pissed, and my dad was disappointed. In the end, it didn't matter because 3 and a half months later I woke up to the most excruciating cramps; feeling the urge to push, I went to the bathroom, and before I knew it, there was my baby. My mom called "the hustler" to inform him of what had just happened and he came from work to pick me up and take me to the hospital. He left the car in the emergency lane, walked in with me, and stayed until I checked in. He told me that he was going to park the car; but instead, he went back to work.

I was livid that missing out on a couple of hours of work was more important than being there for me. *(It wasn't like he really needed the money).* He felt as though his taking me to one of the best hospitals in Chicago would replace his absence. He didn't know it, but while

I was on the bus, I saw him pull his car into the parking lot of the hospital and pull out his phone to call me. I knew he was coming to pick me up; but instead of allowing him to do so, I got on the bus and did not answer any of his calls. I was already sick of his lies and now, I couldn't believe that this man, who said he loved me, left me to deal with the loss of our baby alone. I knew that my love for him wouldn't be the same and shortly after, we broke up; however, it would be a long time before we would fully let each other go.

Can You See Me? *(Written: 2003)*

Can you look at me and see me?
I mean really see me, for who I am, and not just what I can do.
Because see, the way I see you brings tears to my eyes
And my cries, speak to you.

Can you hear me? and really hear me?

Actually hear the sound of my voice and follow my lips,

do you listen?

Do you take what I say in?
because the depth of my words is so strong and so true,
that in reality, you wouldn't know where to begin.

But I hear you, I listen to you,

And my fingertips get cold and there is burning in my soul
Because there is no truth in what you say,

And your eyes hold the key to the conclusion
of your illusion of so-called loving me.

Yet they say actions speak louder than words,
But your eyes...

They tell your life's story.

****

****

-*What About You?*

After that "breakup" and the loss of my baby, I started to think more about my career. By then, I had wasted time attending schools that didn't specialize in what I wanted to do; so, I started looking into schools that did. At the beginning of 2004, I started attending a school for Television and Radio Broadcasting in Lombard, IL. I loved it! I was able to intern for a popular television talk show, as well as a popular production company. One day while in class, the instructor informed us that we would need to produce and host an internet radio station before we could graduate. I wasn't a shy girl, so I asked the first person who looked in my direction if they wanted to partner up. It just so happened that this seemingly quiet guy, whom I had not noticed before, looked in my direction. *"Do you want to be my partner?"* I asked. He responded with a nod and we exchanged phone numbers and started working on our show. We met up at least three times before the day he brought a rose to our session and asked me out on a date; naturally, I accepted.

He was a muscular guy, very attractive, and had a smile that lit up a room. I couldn't believe I hadn't noticed him before. Although I was thrown off by his attire on our first date, *(He wore joggers and a t-shirt)* he was such a gentleman and made me feel safe and comfortable from the very beginning. We became close and he eventually asked me to be in a relationship, I told him I would think about it. *(because things were still pretty complicated with "The Hustler").* After giving it some thought, I decided to finally cut ties with my ex and give *this* man a chance. The day I made that decision though, I found out I was pregnant by my ex once again. We didn't know it at the time; but, neither of us had the mental capacity to be in a relationship at that point in our lives. He was about six years older than I was and things had not gone according to plan in *his* life, and I was pregnant by my ex, still mourning my brother, and still trying to figure out *my own* life.

While in class one day, I began to miscarry for the second time and he took such good care of me. He drove me to the hospital, stayed in the room with me, and made sure I was being treated properly by the medical staff. When I was discharged, he carried me out to the car and into the passenger's seat. I felt so loved and cared for by him all of the time. I felt safe and he matched my sexual energy to the core. He was the first man I had fallen in love with, I gave him ALL I had to give of me, mentally, physically, and sexually. I thought he was my husband, and I had not even thought about marriage before him; nevertheless, he still had his own struggles, and they would spill over into our relationship. We broke up twice before the final break up at the end of 2004. I eventually learned that he didn't make me feel safe and loved *just* because that's how much he loved *me*, he made me feel that way because that was just WHO HE WAS.

We only lasted for nine months, but It took me many years to get over him. I moved away to Springfield because I didn't even want to be in the same city he was in. I wanted to make myself less accessible to him, while I still waited for him to come after me.

What About You? (Written 2004)

Sometimes I think if love, or more so being in love is a choice,
are we together because we choose to be,
or because God put us together?

Anyway,

my feelings towards you have changed,
and while it's a shame,
I still couldn't imagine being without you,
whereas, I don't think you would care either way.

So let's say we part from one another again-
and go in our separate directions and begin our
Inspections of one another's existence in one another's lives,
Can you do without me?

A better question,

Who do you want me to be?

I'm not weak,
And I won't break my neck for you
if you can't break your neck for me,

And my king will be just that, my king,
when I see that I am his queen,
But I don't think you would care either way.

Hopefully one day,

you won't be so cold toward me
And you'll see how much I love you; because I do.

Hopefully, you'll care enough
to actually listen to what I say to you,
Will you do that for me?

Or will it be too late?

****

****

- Terrell Marquis

I was in Springfield for about a year before I moved back home around July of 2005 and started working at Ultra Foods grocery store. I was still not over my heartbreak; however, I was ready to move on. One day this guy called me on my cashier's phone and asked if he could buy me lunch. Later, he asked me for my number and I obliged. He wasn't the typical kind of guy that I would go for, amongst other things, he had braids in his hair, and was only about two and a half years older than I was; but, he was sweet, attentive, and he made what he wanted to be known. We talked on the phone for a couple of weeks before he asked me if he could come over, and once I agreed, he would come over to my parent's house every night after he got off of work, and would always make sure I had gas in my car and lunch for work for the next day.

He and I both were starting our lives over. When I moved back in with my parents after returning from Springfield, I no longer had a room, because my mom had turned it into a nursery for her day-care. I slept on a mattress on the floor of my old bedroom, and after he returned from Iowa, he slept on a futon in his parent's den. He would say, "*I hate coming over here and seeing you have to sleep on the floor, I'm going to get us a crib."* By December 2005, with my parent's help, we moved in together, and by the end of January 2006, I became pregnant. I wanted to give my child a two-parent home and he had shown me that he was a good man; so, when he asked me to marry him, I said yes. We were married in August of 2006, and my baby boy was born a month later. I was a mom, I couldn't believe it! When I became pregnant with my son, I thought for sure I would lose *this* baby since I had lost two before. But when the morning sickness started and my belly began to grow, I knew that this baby wasn't going anywhere, and I secretly started to enjoy every minute of my pregnancy. It was like no love I had ever felt before. Whatever I did/do in life, I always try to put 100% into It, and this was no different. I was *truly* in love. I knew I couldn't teach my son how to be a man, but I was damn sure going to teach him what *kind* of man to be.

Terrell Marquis (Written: 2006)

When I first met you, I was more than pleased-
At mommy's strong man, stronger than, Hercules.
then, eventually, I became very afraid,
A- young man in a world full of violence and gangs,
of- people who will test the person in you,
by-
picking and provoking just to see what you'll do,
so,
I-as your mother, have to teach you to be strong,
when-
you feel like you're falling, you have to hold on,
When-
you feel you're being tested, just simply walk away,

And be a man of your word always do what you say,
And say what you'll do and make sure it gets done,
And Don't doubt yourself or judge anyone.
But-
for now, just keep being my baby boy,
And keep filling my life with happiness and joy,
and tears when you smile so beautifully,
A love so strong, so deep within me - I
never knew existed until I looked in your eyes
You-
Filled a hole in my heart that came when pooh died
My-son-
My joy, my piece of me, my love, my all and everything-
Mommy loves you so much....

-Terrell Marquis

****

****

-Briana Marie

I began having weird episodes after my son was born. I was angry and depressed a lot because even though I loved my baby, I really wanted more for myself than a 1-bedroom apartment, no job, and no degree. My son had me so sick during my pregnancy, that I lost my job working for a mailroom company in downtown Chicago. I had to depend on my husband and that was something I was not used to. I would be so sad, then so angry, and all of those emotions fell solely upon my husband. I knew that something was wrong; so, I went to the doctor and was diagnosed with post-partum depression and prescribed medication. I didn't want to take the medication; so, instead of picking the prescription up from the pharmacy, I decided that my condition came from my not being where I pictured in life, and since I understood what was going on with me mentally, I was able to tackle it by focusing more on my happy baby, enrolling in college and praying.

Side Note: Focusing on my baby, enrolling in college, and praying worked for me during that horrific time; however, if you are a woman struggling with post-partum depression, please do whatever is healthy for you and your family.

Around the end of 2007, I became pregnant again and my poor husband yet again had to deal with a psychotic wife. My hormones were all over the place, I had become aggressive, depressed, and angry at him because at that time, I did not want another child and we sure as hell couldn't afford it. I had just started working and was financially taking care of us on my own after my husband lost his job. We were struggling and waiting for an eviction notice to surface on our door; so, It was definitely not a good time to have a baby.

I was about 4 and a half months pregnant when I went to get an ultrasound and found out I was having a girl. I asked the technician to double-check at least 3 times, *"Are you sure?!"* I asked excitingly. Once he verified for the third time that I was indeed having a girl, I was on cloud nine and called my mom right away. *"Ma! Guess who's having a girl?!"*

"Who?" she asked. *"Oh my gosh ma meeeeeee!",* I answered.

My excitement turned into sheer panic once I thought about how the hell I was going to raise a girl when I myself wasn't a "girly girl". I was 23 years old and had my hair done maybe 3 times in my life, and my nails done once for my 8th-grade luncheon and graduation, what was I going to teach her about being a "girl"?

Then on May 29, 2008, I went into labor, and when this absolutely gorgeous little lady came into my life, I learned that I didn't need to be girly to teach her- her worth, self-respect, cleanliness, and strength. Ironically, as she started to get older, I learned that my little girl wasn't a "girly girl" either.

Briana Marie (Written: 2008)

When I found out about you, I admit, I was a little confused,
I mean,
I've never been a "girly girl"; so,
would I even know what to do?
But then, you came out reminding me so much of ME,
I couldn't bear to put you down.
I kept you wrapped in my arms from morning til' night -
That's probably why you're so spoiled now.
My-
beautiful princess,
whom I must protect, and also teach right from wrong,
Teach you not only how to be a lady,
but as a woman, you must be strong.
To instill in you your worth,
which is more expensive than diamonds and gold,
To teach you to be loving, caring, and independent,
because your hand forever-
I cannot hold.
But right now,
just keep being my baby girl, my princess, and best friend
And
Be my sun that shines bright in the morning,

a light- that does not end.
My-
daughter, my heart, my life, and the air I breathe,
My love, my cookie, my everything,
My accomplishment...

Briana Marie~

****

****

- Cancer

It would be almost 10 years before I wrote another poem. During that time, my parents separated, then divorced; my dad remarried, and my mom became engaged. My children were getting older and requiring my attention differently at every stage of their lives and I was too busy raising them to write. It wasn't until we lost two of my husband's relatives whom I adored, to cancer- that I found my way back to God and my voice in writing again. I wrote a poem where I depicted cancer as a serial killer with no remorse; however, I will be taking this moment to rewrite that poem based on more personal experiences with the disease. In 2018, my grandmother died of cancer, and last year in 2022, my dad was diagnosed with cancer.

When my grandmother died, my mom and aunts had already left the facility to complete the funeral arrangements, and I was at work when I felt strongly in my spirit to get to the hospice facility. I kept hearing "LEAVE NOW", and after the second more authoritative "LEAVE NOW," I left, and It was just my grandmother and me when she took her last breath.

When my dad's cancer diagnosis was confirmed, I stayed in bed for days trying to cope. I felt as though it was unfair for me to continue to live my life while my dad was going through such an ordeal. I would see my kids out for school, be there to talk to them about their day, cook dinner, and lie back in bed. On the weekends, I would barely leave the bed at all. One day, my husband made me get out of bed to take a ride with him, and all I could do was cry. I kept trying to figure out, how I would live without my dad. I prayed for healing for him, and strength for him and our family. Then, the Lord told me he was going to be okay. I didn't know if that meant that my dad would be with HIM in Glory, or if it meant that he was going to be healed. Either way, if God says it, whatever it means, I was trusting in the Lord, because all things happen according to HIS will. My Holy Father gave me the strength to endure and I put my armor on and began to pray, praise, and worship God and encouraged my dad to continue to do the same. Even though my dad didn't fully complete his treatments, as of 04/2023, my dad is cancer free.

Greater is HE who is above ALL THINGS!

Cancer (Written 03/2023)

Cancer is a monster-
 who does not care about your age,
your social-economic status, your looks, or your race,
And, we live in a world today
where cures are kept secret and
Money making is key,
So-
People are getting pumped with medications
 that could kill them for a fee?

Cancer is a monster,
With no regard for human life,
radiation and chemo making them too weak to fight,
too hurt to move, and too angry to pray,
not looking or feeling like themselves due to
constantly losing weight,
Not
Eating or, sleeping
And, worrying about the people they love
whom-
they're not ready to leave.
but see,
Cancer may be a monster- but Jesus is King!
And it is HE who has dominion over everything-
So-
don't ever let fear overpower your faith, and-
fight with HIM boldly by your side
and, if it's in HIS will for you to take your heavenly place,
Then-Remember...
there are no goodbyes.

****

****

- Love without Losing Yourself

I was 22 and my husband was 24 years old when we got married. At the beginning of my marriage, my husband would come all the way to downtown Chicago to pick me up from work, just to take me to my car a block away. Other times, I would come home from work to rose petals spread across the floor, from the front door to the bathroom- where there would be a hot candlelit bathtub full of bubbles waiting for me. He wouldn't go to the corner store without bringing me something back.

He was always thinking of me and was a great boyfriend and then-husband. He would hold my umbrella when it rained, tie my shoes, dress and undress me, and wash, blow-dry, and flat iron my hair. He supported me and took care of our babies while I completed my Associate's and Bachelor's degrees, and would keep them quiet while I would be studying. He did so much for me in the beginning that I would joke, *"Baby, can you bring me the toilet? I have to use the restroom,"* and he would say *"Let me get my tools."*

We were each other's rocks and supported one another through whatever we would be doing and/or going through. One year, my husband lost his job and the ability to provide for his family for a second time. Everything fell on me again financially; but this time, I wasn't as understanding or supportive. Things gradually started to change, and seven or eight years into our marriage, alcohol crept in and turned my husband into a totally different person.

He became disconnected and was home less and less and I was left raising our two kids alone while also being disrespected and disregarded. I genuinely commend all the single mothers out there; but, when you are married and have to *live* like you're a single mother, that is a *whole* different type of feeling. He was out of work for a couple of years before he got another job and took over all the bills, but the drinking didn't stop; in fact, it got worse. We separated several times throughout this time period, but when the drinking would pause-I would see the man I once had and hit the resume button on the relationship. I tried to understand his addiction because I had an addiction of my own. It angered me that I was fighting my own addiction while he was enjoying his. Still, I wanted to make sure I did EVERYTHING I could before giving up on my marriage, so I began to pray over him while he slept and anoint his head and feet with holy oil. I asked the Lord to make the taste miserable for him so that he would no longer desire it. My Life became about pushing and chasing my husband and raising my children to be God-fearing people with goals, values, and integrity, I was filling up everyone else's cup, while mine was empty. I was depleted.

Along the way, I began to distract myself; because I desperately needed to feel like ME. I didn't realize that my own distractions were delaying my blessings, and things got really bad in 2018 when my husband betrayed me in the most profound way. I won't go into too much depth, but let me just say that there are things that are far worse than cheating, and when he didn't have my back when members of his immediate family began making up lies about me and attacking my character, I cleared my head by getting rid of my *own* distractions and 3 months later in 2019, I made the decision to file for divorce. While I myself was not perfect, I knew that I didn't deserve what he was putting me through, and after I decided that it was time for me to find ME again, I knew that this time, I wasn't going to lose HER for anyone.

Love Without Losing Yourself (Written 2019)

Learning to love without Losing yourself,
That, I'm pretty sure most women can understand,
Especially those of us in relationships
Who've-
Given so much to a man And-
Let's not talk about how we try to make them
feel how much we give By-

Pulling it from down deep in our core,
And when they try not to see, or choose not to believe it,
You lose yourself more and more and for what?
No appreciation from a selfish love,- better yet
Sis
You're being taken advantage of-
All because of the potential you think you see
Saying: I GAVE TO YOU WHAT I TOOK OUT OF ME
And now you're trying to figure out why they can't
love you -the same way - you love them
Why-
You care so much and they seem to not give a damn.
Excusing their actions because you're not quite ready to-
let them go,
Asking yourself what is all of this for-
meanwhile-
you lose yourself more and more -
until there isn't any of you left-
you're just a shell of a person who once was -
You can't even recognize yourself.
Learn to love without losing yourself,
for the unselfish person, this may difficult to do
But once your patience has reached an end-
only then you can comprehend,
That no one
Can love you, more than YOU.

****

****

- Marriage

By the end of 2019, my prayers had been answered and my husband started to slowly began seeking the Lord again; so, I put the divorce on hold. Soon after, the drinking slowed down tremendously. We closed on our first home; and with his support, I obtained a Master's degree. In 2022, the drinking started to creep its' ugly head again, but this time, I was a different ME, and I knew what I wanted and would no longer accept. My husband and I share the same sentiments about marriage; so, once I expressed those things to him, he did what was required to save his marriage, and in 2022, the drinking stopped completely. Now, he has fully given himself to the Lord, and not only did he stop drinking, he also stopped smoking, and cursing too. He hears my needs, and I can tell that he is going to God concerning our marriage. We still have some scars that are healing on both our ends; however, we still love each other and believe in marriage, and through everything we put each other through, we are still looking forward to growing old and babysitting our grandchildren together.

In marriage, there are good times and bad times; but, I learned that it's a process that operates more smoothly with God, and if the two of you truly love one another and are committed to making the marriage work, getting through the tough times can be a rewarding experience.

Marriage (Written 6/2023)

Marriage is not easy, I mean,
It is not a piece of cake, like,
Working at it and loving each other
Is a decision you'll have to make every day.

And-

Saying for rich or for poorer -
is easier said than done,
And in sickness and in health sounds good-
Until one of yawl health is gone.

And speaking of sickness, let's expound on that bit because -
Sickness can mean more than your typical disease,
See-
Sickness can also be an affliction like an addiction and
all of its obscurities.

Marriage is forgiving,
Because you both will change with time
and-I'm not just talking about your looks and your body,
I'm referring to your heart and your mind –
because, believe me,
You will change, and
 someone might struggle to find their place,
So-
That's when the other has to allow room for you to grow

While -
also displaying patience and grace.

Marriage is work,
But it can be a beautiful thing- like
The pillow talks and partnerships, the-
Never taking off your rings,
the Family, the support, the love,
The two souls becoming of one, the-
Passion, the playfulness, the friendship,
the sitting around and just having fun-
the-
building of a family- of a legacy,
I mean,
It is really truly an art,
So-
Marriage may not be easy,
But-
Til' death may do its part.

****

****

THAT'S IT, THAT'S ALL

If my life had of went according to *my* plan, I would have graduated from high school with high honors, gone to my dream College University, and had a career as a television producer for somebody's TV show if not my own. I used to get so depressed about life because I wasn't where I wanted to be. Now, I look at my family; my husband, and my beautiful children, and I can see how God used me and continues to use me for his Glory in their lives as well as my own. I will not ever lose myself again, but this process has shown me: that I can keep evolving as Shawana, and still be a wife and mom at the same time.

While looking back brought back so many memories and emotions, I learned that those memories and emotions are what made me who I am today. I want to conclude this memoir with a teachable moment-as my kids would call it- It's okay to remember the past, just don't stay there too long pondering on what would have, could have, or should have been. **Isaiah 43:18-19 says *"Remember ye, not the former things, neither consider things of old, behold, I will do a new thing.*** If your life is not where you want it right now, trust in the Lord and change it.

I truly hope that you enjoyed reading my poetry and the real-life experiences that birthed them; because I truly enjoyed getting back to my passion for writing.

May God continue to bless you in all of your lives and in all that
you may do.

Love,

Shawana

The End